T0345844

Once upon a time...

MONSTERPIECES

of the 2000s!

ORO *editions*
Publishers of Architecture, Art, Design and Photography
Gordon Goff - Publisher
USA: PO Box 998, Pt Reyes Station, CA 94956
Asia: Block 8, Lorong Bakar Batu #02-04 Singapore 348743
www.oroeditions.com
info@oroeditions.com

Copyright © 2010 by ORO *editions*

ISBN: 978-0-9819857-3-2

Additional Graphic Design: Davina Tjandra
Production and Project Coordination: Joanne Tan and Davina Tjandra
Color Separation and Printing: ORO *group* Ltd

ORO *editions* has made every effort to minimize the carbon footprint of this project.
In pursuit of this goal, ORO *editions*, in association with Global ReLeaf, has arranged
to plant two trees for each and every tree used in the manufacturing of the FSC paper
produced for this book. Global ReLeaf is an international campaign run by American
Forests, the nation's oldest nonprofit conservation organization. Global ReLeaf is
American Forests' education and action program that helps individuals, organizations,
agencies, and corporations improve the local and global environment by planting and
caring for trees.

To our generation of architecture lovers and their children;
to our generation of architects and their built creatures.

ACKNOWLEDGEMENTS

An Independent Study course at Harvard Graduate School of Design, led by Sanford Kwinter and Michael Kubo, marked the genesis of this book in August 2008. As Master in Architecture students, we spent days (and nights) at neighboring desks in studio. Such proximity and a common sensibility gave birth to the project. Beginning with chats that grew into serious discussions and research on iconic contemporary buildings, we decided that rather than keeping it to ourselves, we wanted to be heard. We were exploring innovative ways to communicate to our fellow architects and the general public. The oscillation between admiration and rebellion sparked the creative process of this global collaborative work. Five thousand eight hundred seventy-four e-mails later, *Monsterpieces* was born and ready for publication.

In essence, we wanted to shoot a small arrow to the untouchable, searching for their Achilles' heel and doing so in the most penetrating way. We soon realized the difficulty and perseverance that were necessary for first-time publishing, and are grateful for the intellectual and emotional support we received from each other.

Sanford Kwinter advised us through the formation period of the project. We are grateful for the unconventional discussions and approach, and the time we spent exploring materials everywhere from bestiaries to horror movies, and especially the narrative organizational matrix of James Joyce's *Ulysses*. Michael Kubo patiently gave us his generous advice and time, sharing with us numerous references. His resourcefulness regarding architecture books and the publishing market gave us a clearer picture early in the process.

This book covers a timely subject. Through a challenging and exciting process, it has elicited enthusiastic responses and discussions from Princeton and Harvard faculty and students. Many professors have critiqued, inspired (sometimes indirectly), advised, helped, and encouraged us to accelerate the publication of the book. Our thanks goes to Ed Eigen, Lars Muller, Lluis Ortega, and Hashim Sarkis. Rafael Moneo's encouraging advice was particularly helpful. Melissa Vaughn, of the Harvard GSD publishing department, and Eric Howeler, who also teaches at the GSD, gave us invaluable advice on publishing in architecture. Our classmate and friend, Ricardo Camacho, gave his candid and constructive advice as usual, and helped clarify our direction in producing a retrospective of a new form of functionalism. Professors at Princeton and Harvard, including Scott Cohen, Jesse Reiser, and Eve Aschheim—always influential and thought-provoking figures to us in many ways— constantly reminded us of the sublimity in curiosity and the intensity in clarity of thought.

We thank Dean Ralph Lerner and Vivi Ying He of the University of Hong Kong, who offered to introduce us to Chinese language publishers. Leslie Burke, Deniz McGee, and Janice Harvey were very helpful in later stage coordination. We thank Francois Chaslin for his radio program that shares his architectural vision and helps many, including us, to increase our architectural knowledge every Wednesday; we especially thank him for his assistance in searching for French publishers. We are enormously grateful to Monica Ponce de Leon for her help in connecting us with ORO *editions*. Amid her tight schedule as dean, professor, architect, wife, and mother, she has shown unremitting support and encouragement from the very start.

A special thanks goes to our publisher, ORO *editions*, who has chosen to believe in this project by two young architects. Taking the risk of investment to promote new voices in the arts, Gordon Goff deserves our profound gratitude. We also thank Joanne Tan and Davina Aryani Tjandra for their continuous collaboration with us in publishing *Monsterpieces*.

The contributors to this book are exceptionally generous, passionate, and encouraging about the topic. Antoine Picon has given us his continuous advice and criticism since the birth of the project, and has opened our eyes to our own Koolhaasian subjectivity. We are grateful for his interest in our project and his enthusiasm for Surrealism. Spyros Papapetros, extremely knowledgeable in Surrealism, has always influenced us with his intellectual intensity and energy, and his incessant interest in animal architecture and monsters. Thanks to Timothy Hyde, who organized the seminar History of the Future, sharing some similar ideas as well as one of the best discussions on the book. Jonathan Solomon kindly gave us sufficient pages in the journal *306090* (Issue 13: Sustain & Develop) for a book preview, as well as testing grounds for our ideas, frequent advice, sharing of experience, and friendship.

We are indebted to the three deans—Stan Allen, Ralph Lerner, and Mohsen Mostafavi—who wrote the endorsements. Having them together on the cover of a book is of historical importance; we can only hope the content of *Monsterpieces* is powerful enough not to be eclipsed.

Special thanks also goes to Jan-Emmanuel De Neve for his continuous advice (he remains Aude-Line's most intricate and fascinating monster case study), and Anne Wittmann and Pol-Andre Duliere for their unfailing support.

And thanks, as always, to Susan Lam, who volunteered her time in proofreading and "proofviewing," Grace and Paul Wong for their ineffable assistance in all the important little things. Their patience, insight, and support have made this project possible.

Finally, our gratitude to the architects, builders, parents, and conceivers of all the creatures explored in this book, without whom our generation would not have crossed this stimulating architectural period and without whom this book would not have seen the light. Our inspiration emanates from their projects and legacy.

12 December, 2009
London, UK / Hong Kong, China

FOREWORD:
Future Transactions

Timothy W. Hyde

efore entering into this speculative collection of architectural futures, one should perhaps recollect the mythological figure Cassandra, who could foretell the future, but whose prophecies no one believed: When Cassandra appears in the first play of the *Oresteia*, she hesitates to enter Agamemnon's palace because she sees the bloody past of the family as vividly as if she had witnessed its occurrence. Cassandra also sees the future; she sees that Clytemnestra will murder both her and Agamemnon. The chorus tells Cassandra that they are perplexed by the uncanny accuracy of her account of past events and mystified by her (to them) incomprehensible account of future events. Cassandra responds by saying that her inability to persuade them does not matter, and that what will be, will be. Then, knowing her own fate, Cassandra enters the palace and is killed.

The myth of Cassandra distills the fatalistic belief that individuals will not influence a preordained destiny ready to take its course, but it contains another parallel implication quite relevant to the following catalogue of monsterpieces. Standing before the palace vainly describing the events that have and that will transpire there, Cassandra *represents* these events. That is to say, when Cassandra prophesies the future, she produces with her words the semblance of that future in the present. The appearance of the future as a semblance in the present is quite distinct from the fulfillment of that future. It is actually the semblance rather than the future that is instrumental, the semblance that creates meaning by contextualizing in sharp relief the value of present actions, interactions, decisions, and motives. But since those who hear it refuse to be persuaded by the semblance that Cassandra conjures, is it not best described as a representation of the future that is simultaneously a failure to represent?

Cassandra and her fate thus reveal at least two crucial understandings to be borne along as one explores the monsterpieces: first, that these carefully devised acts of prediction must be approached as representational transactions in the present, substitutions of one coherent view by another; and second, that the assessment of accuracy they seem overtly to solicit accompanies a more discreet strategy of persuasion. The purpose of this bestiary is to enable a different view of our own present refracted through a set of possible futures, to enable a distinctively contemporary view, in the sense of a perspective at once within and removed from its temporal present.

One presumption to be resisted, then, would be the acceptance of the monsterpieces as mere critiques of a present moment of architecture, as revelations of various insufficiencies in the buildings whose futures they imagine. Another presumption, as easy to fall into as the first, would be to regard the bestiary as an intellectual quarantine of a periodic recurrence of a formalist or intuitionalist tendency that has not proved susceptible to any of the vaccinations tested thus far. Each of these presumptions adopts the familiar expectations of architectural critique, the deconstruction of an occurrence all too easy to predict.

And so, if one successfully sets aside these presumptions, what foreknowledge do the monsterpieces then reveal? That Modernism's never too firm grasp of the indexical possibility of form has sheared irrevocably away from the postmodern evolution of its techniques of production...that the indulgence of architectural desires is a predictably fleeting satisfaction unsuited to the medium's temporal duration...that life can constrain architecture but that architecture cannot constrain life? Each is a valid and necessary statement, although the last, admittedly, is a prognosis that in the past has gone largely unremarked, with the exception of a small number of architects who have tried, unsuccessfully, to fully accede to its implications.

But perhaps, like Cassandra's predicted future, the foreknowledge does not conclude the story, but initiates it. Each monsterpiece is a semblance of a possible future, devised neither to congratulate the present moment nor to condemn it. Each monsterpiece aims, instead, to displace the present moment, to substitute a new origin in place of the old. For once the bestiary is known, it forestalls the naïve return to the conceptions and beliefs that commenced the evolution of these elaborate forms and complex environments. The bestiary effects a representational transaction in which a speculative future supersedes the determined past. The curtailment of that past resonates as a critique, but its supersession could be regarded as a renovation.

Each reader will need to be open to the possibility of discovering in the pages of the bestiary new valuations, new temporalities, or new virtualities. Like any children's story, a cautionary tale draws its suspenseful strength from the persuasive powers of the objects of temptation. The monsterpieces are less imaginings of failures of an architectural moment than reimaginings of a present potential. Are these monsterpieces warnings or seductions? In Cassandra's words: what will be, will be.

INTRODUCTION:
On Monstrosity
in Our Dystopian Representation
of Contemporary Architecture

Just as psychoanalysis reconstructs the original traumatic situation in order to release the repressed material, so we are now being plunged back into the archaeopsychic past, uncovering the ancient taboos and drives that have been dormant for epochs...Each one of us is as old as the entire biological kingdom, and our bloodstreams are tributaries of the great sea of its total memory.

J.G. Ballard [1]

Speculations

This book is a retrospective manifesto of contemporary architecture as monstrous organisms with transient actors. It speculates on whether the social ecology[2] that many iconic buildings claim to address remains sustainable after years. It contemplates ecological reforms that reshape the anatomy of these buildings. In a time of architectural uncertainty and digital revolution, we use children's graphics to tell the story of contemporary architectural icons.

Buildings today are accelerated in regeneration, constructed for temporal needs.[3] What happens when these constructed objects persist in time? What if there is no booming economy to replace them? What if another type of program appropriation occurs; how would the users behave?

These graphic explorations focus on such speculative futures. We show not only what the future forms of buildings will be, but also, possible adaptations by their users. These speculations glorify the absurdity of architectural forms in the 2000s. They underscore the consequent implications in building permanence and resistance. Contemporary buildings

[1] J.G. Ballard, *The Drowned World* (Orion Millennium, 1999), 41.

[2] Vittoria Di Palma, Diana Periton, Marina Lathouri, *Intimate Metropolis: Urban Subject in the Modern City* (Routledge, 2008).

[3] Moshen Mostafavi and David Leatherbarrow, *On Weathering: The Life of Building in Time* (MIT Press, 1993), 23.

appear to have strong, persistent forms in imagery, but weak reliance on any one program. The pretentious hyper-rationalization of "form follows program" is a myth to begin with. The permanence of these forms paradoxically offers low resistance to any new program.

How will these buildings outlive the period for which they have been intended?

> It is not the strongest of the species that survives, nor the most intelligent that survives. It is the one that is the most adaptable to change.
>
> **Charles Darwin**

> I consider it useless and tedious to represent what exists, because nothing that exists satisfies me. Nature is ugly, and I prefer the monsters of my fancy to what is positively trivial.
>
> **Charles Baudelaire** [4]

Iconic Ruins

ur gaze is evocative of the appropriation of **ruins**—of the ancient pyramids as well as of future ruins. What could be the result of such a population, willing to conserve iconic structures by appropriated programs?

In this book, the definition of "monster" lies in the fact that there is no mediation between the huge scale of urban iconic forms and the tiny, bacteriological scale of the human. Observations in the clash of scales between these icons and their inhabitants lead to reflections on Lefebvre. If Lefebvre's social space is a means of control, domination, power, and reflection of social relations[5], what does monstrous architecture tell us about social spaces today?

We create caricatures of contemporary architecture as monsters in the Modern and Postmodern families. Monsters imply a tension between consanguinity and anomaly, a

---

[4] Charles Baudelaire, *Art in Paris 1845–1862*, trans. Jonathan Mayne (Oxford, 1965), 155.
[5] Henri Lefebvre, *The Production of Space* (1974).

11

balance between architecture's self-referentiality and its concern with producing social spaces expressive of the zeitgeist. Monsters are by nature the anomaly in the family, the black sheep. Like a mule, which is bred from a horse and a donkey and cannot reproduce, contemporary architecture tends to be a hybrid of its historical precedents. Destined to be lonely creatures, mass reproduction of the monster turns it into the norm, where it loses its fantastic monstrosity.

Embracing Dystopia

derivative of the survival of the fittest, the book narrates the fictional transformation of the non-adapted to the hegemony of the super-adapted.

Our apotropaic operation references the proto-surgical encyclopedic survey in the Middle Ages that taxonomically exhibits the anomalies and strangeness of entities that derive from both reality and the imagination.

In Medieval bestiaries, animals are interpreted following the Bible or conventional wisdom, possibly as a means to digest the state of human coexistence with these strange creatures. Providing a survey of monsters, the Medieval stories speak about the animals as actors of a set, depicting the particularities and performances of the animals in relation to myth and religion. These iconic animals are used as symbols to communicate notions of good and bad, paradise and hell. It is interesting to note that the symbolic meanings of these animals are not reduced to fast, diagrammatic images; rather, they remain ambiguous. For instance, the lion and the dragon are both good and bad; they can be the protectors of the gates, but also the incarnation of evil. The stories are not only descriptive of form, but also of behavior, by the use of allegories.

The bestiaries ignore geographical limits, choosing to depict a global situation. Animals from everywhere are mixed in the same set. In Medieval Europe, the elephant was as exotic and fantastic as the dragon.

Like the Medieval bestiaries, this book adopts the method of apotropaic representation and the attitude of judgmental acceptance. The set of buildings chosen is a repository of contemporary architectural anomalies, not unlike formaldehyde containers of embalmed architecture.

L'euefque de mer.

La terre n'a euefques feulement,
Qui font par bulé en grád hōneur & tiltre,
L'euefque croiſt en mer femblablement,
Ne parlát point, cōbien qu'il porte mitre.

Le Ciclope.

De Polipheme & des Siclopiens,
Font mention poetes anciens:
On dit encor que ce lignage dûre,
Auec vn œil felon ceſte figure.

Le Cyclope et L'évêque de mer.
Desprez, Francois. *Recueil de la diversité des habits, qui sont de present en usage, tant es pays d'Europe, Asie, Affrique & Isles sauvages, le tout fait apres le naturel.* Paris: Richard Breton,1564.
Courtesy of Bibliothèque Municipale de Tours. by ©BM de Tours (Bibliothèque Municipale de Tours)

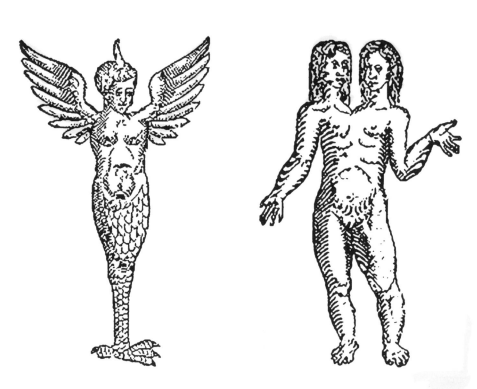

The monster of Ravenne.
Paré Ambroise. *Des monstres et prodiges.* Paris: G. Buon, 1585.
© BIUM (Bibliothèque Interuniversitaire de Médecine et d'odontologie-Paris)

If accepted, the monstrous loses its monstrosity. The monstrosity effect is ephemeral; its enemy is the conventional, which transforms strangeness into normality. Each case of monstrosity questions humanity (Siam Brothers); it is polemical and of public interest. It is surely a valid claim that mankind has a natural attraction for monstrosity. The feeling mixes curiosity with the uncanny, and complexity with the *jouissance* not to be the object of curiosity.

The "sublime" neighbors the "intriguing"—are architects exploiting the attraction for monstrosity, using the creation of an artificial strangeness as a strategy for architectural attention from the public?

Frankenstein architectures are experiments where the creator does not anticipate the interaction of his avatar with the world. Once the building gets its autonomy, it opens the door to unpredicted behaviors and futures.

The post-processing of the notion of "form follows function" in the 2000s underlines the phenomenon that produces forms irrelevant to their intrinsic functional needs, involving unadapted interior generic space that works for any function, or "junkspace."[6] Their shapes only respond to the desire of manifesting themselves as strong silhouettes in the skyline, the wish for self-expression, as monsters. Monsters are noticeable and call for attention; their form optimizes the function of showing. With an arguable relationship to aesthetics and ornament, buildings of our times have created architectural tumors, hypertrophies of deformed features—artifacts that do not respond to any need or function but act only as manifestation.

We are witnesses to the anomaly of monsterpieces. The misinterpretation of our architecture helps us to understand, glorify, and critique the absurdity of the current hypertrophied architectural organs.

The depiction of these buildings in a dystopian stage projects us into an imaginable future. The idea of pathology enhances its hidden fragility, and the mode of destruction of the monster is contained within itself. Through this dystopian vision, we question the future of architecture, and particularly, the aftermath of the hegemony of the major buildings that map the architectural landscape of our times. In the spirit of informal economy, the book offers a lighthearted critique of contemporary iconic buildings.

---

[6] Rem Koolhaas, "Junkspace." Chuihua Judy Chung, Jeffrey Inaba et al, eds. *Harvard School of Design Guide to Shopping* (Taschen, 2002).

The pelican: A bird that revives its dead young with its own blood.
Pelicanus, Den Haag, Museum Meermanno-Westreenianum, 10 B 25., produced in France, c. 1450
Courtesy of Museum Meermanno

> Adversity makes men, and prosperity makes monsters.
>
> **Victor Hugo**

Antinomy: Functionalist Iconicity & "Form Follows Form"

s representation, the monster is an invention that functions as society's critic; as performing object, the monster is dysfunctional in its own reality (think Frankenstein the novel character vs. Frankenstein *in* the novel). Monsters are different from machines, which Modernist architecture evokes. Machines have components that work well together; monsters have parts that hardly work together. Machines are healthy and fit; monsters are barely functional. Unlike collage, which implies looseness in the combination of things, the monster's sutured pieces cannot be taken apart easily. Paradoxically, it is this innate incompatibility that glues it into a ridiculous yet iconic whole.

The criticism in the book implies the personification of iconic buildings, at least in terms of classification of characters. Nevertheless, these buildings are accustomed to figural narration and humanization, and are often referred to by nicknames. Torre Agbar is known for having a phallic character, and by several nicknames, such as "*el supositori*" (the suppository) or "*l'obús*" (the shell). The *Berlaymonster* in Brussels refers to the fortress-like local EU Headquarters[7]. The CCTV complex in Beijing is the subject of jokes about the building's resemblance to "Big Underpants" (大裤衩)and its proposed nickname. "Knowledge Window," (智窗, *zhichuang*) should really be the homophone "hemorrhoids."[8] These denigrating nicknames arguably attack, or reinforce, their proud silhouettes.

The representations in this book demonstrate that many of today's architectural icons can essentially be communicated through children's graphics. Legible to developing minds, books for young children offer simplified representations of the world. Curiously, the simplified representations in this book do not differ much from the reality of the built works. This points to the reducibility of contemporary architecture to its diagrams. The laziness of taking the means as an end produces legible diagrams as icons that sell the project in competitions and to clients. Spatial experience, given its complexity and illegibility, is predictably a bad promotion tool. Shouldn't the architectural diagram be a simplified representation of a sophisticated reality, rather than the direct translation of a simplified reality?

[7] John Tagliabue, "A Bubble of Diplomats and Officials is Set to Pop," *The New York Times*, http://www.nytimes.com/2009/06/23/world/europe/23brussels.html?scp=1&sq=brussels++Berlaymonster&st=nyt (June 22, 2009).

[8] "Rem Koolhaas and CCTV Architecture Porn," *Danwei*, http://www.danwei.org/architecture/rem_koolhaas_and_cctv_porn.php (August 20, 2009).

Post-Occupancy of the Monster
& the Archiology of the 2000s!

Looking back from the future, the graphics and texts narrate, in a factual and naïve manner, the future state of iconic buildings. Referencing anatomical drawings of monsters and other creatures in the bestiaries, the monster buildings are treated as archaeological specimens of the future. Like the bestiaries, our stories come in the form of rumors, reports, and conjectures about these monsterpieces.

The drawings underscore the absurdity of creating incredible shapes. They represent the work of future archaeologists and paleontologists exploring a current architectural trend. Ignoring the hegemony of iconicity as the main generator of architectural form and urban silhouette, the archaeologists attempt to explain these shapes from a rational and functional point of view, overlooking iconicity as irrational fetish. This gaze in the post-process drawings brings us to the imaginative world, which underestimates the aim of these shapes to respond to their urban environment as icons. What if these incredible forms were generated from the inside, to respond to their particular functions? Our post-rationalization challenges contemporary architecture that offers quasi-random iconic forms to the city yet contradicts its interior uses, relating our criticism to the notion of junkspace, as well as the pretentious hyper-rationalization of "form follows program." In other words, the book points out the peculiar relationships between contemporary forms and their programs.

To magnify our point, our imaginary future archaeologists are assumed to have ignored the consequences of Postmodernism and have based the notion of iconicity on the Modernist period. They know iconicity only as the consequence of forms that optimize functions, ignoring iconicity as the aim—urban figures that can be stuffed with whatever filling. Taking the examples of a chimney in an industrial city and a watertower in New York, iconicity has often been the consequence of the structures' functions.

In Darwinian evolution and paleontology, the features of animals' bodies are also shaped to optimize their functions. An atrophied organ with no apparent purpose or endogenously demonstrated need—such as the remaining tail of a bear or the wings of the ostrich—is left for speculation on its former use. This jump in architectural evolution, in which developed hypertrophied features unresponsive to any function other than being or showing, results in what is considered the abnormal or the deviant. Our speculation extrapolates functions from such shapes. After "form follows function" comes the perverse, consanguine loop, where form follows... form. Our taxonomy from an archaeological vision narrates a contemporary state of architecture.

What was this?

A Headquarters

Destroyed shortly after construction. In the Blue
Revolution, the People built the structure to establish
their laboratory at the top. The ellipsoid shape was
perfect for raising the war cyborg. It grew in a controlled
environment while benefiting from the heat produced
by the greenhouse effect of the tower.
Torre Agbar, Barcelona

What was this?

A Beach

Many would come and bathe in KASAdaMU SCIKHA, a strong and heavy tectonic plate to resist the strength of the waves. At the time it was built, ropoд was not yet colonized by the Russians, and this structure was still at large in the Atlantic. It was proven that its function is to conserve the autumn seawater throughout the year. Indeed, the Portuguese had discovered that the autumn toxin production of mussels gives seawater medicinal value.

Casa da Musica, Porto

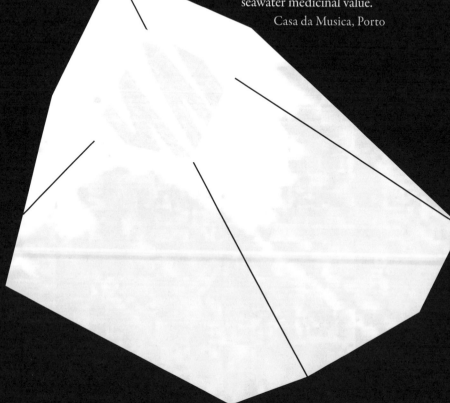

What was this?

A Recycling Center

This structure was a pioneering waste management system in its time. All metal waste was forwarded from this steel nest. The robots managing the system were old robots reused from the car production industry. The structure, made of multiple rails aiming in all directions, allowed for flexibility of garbage displacement.
National Stadium, Beijing

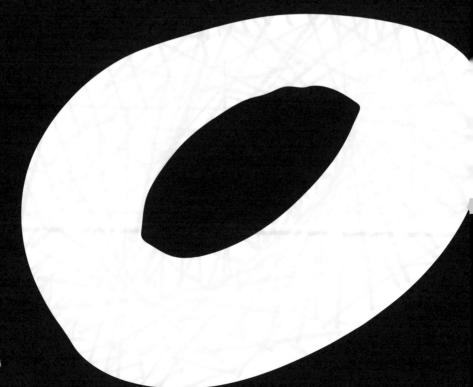

One of the first attempts by humans to create clouds. The clouds were produced to communicate with the satellites floating around the Earth. At that time the settlement on the moon was not yet established as the permanent White House. The clouds were produced at regular intervals and once loaded with gas will take off and...
Blur Building, Yverdon-les-Bains

What was this?

An Aquarium

What was this?

A Greenhouse

Some academics made correlations between this structure and other ruins around the world where gigantic prismatic volumes have been reported. The question remains: why would people in the 21st century need so much empty space in a glass volume? Some say it was for atmosphere storage. Others believe in the myth of social gatherings. Some even surmise on the potential storage of books.

Public Library, Seattle

What was this?

A Swimming Pool

Studies by social historians concluded that dog-swimming was a popular activity in the early stages of the Pet-Obsession Period (POP). Connections were made with the inverted demographic pyramid, where children started to disappear from the population. While the remaining children used the pool during the day, dog-swimming and gambling benefit from the facility with opening hours of 24/7.

Sharp Center for Design, Toronto

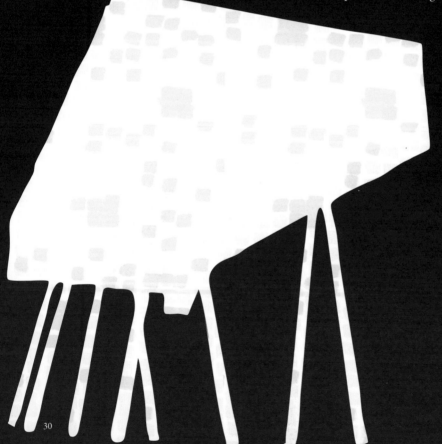

31

What was this?

A Hospital

Its strange envelope has been witnessed on an Asian island. People have reported that the enclosed structure offered no means of opening. Newborns displayed complications due to the scarcity of oxygen and saturation of airborne particles. As a result, they were put in special equipment inside this closed structure. An anonymous source, however, reported that psychological instability was common for both mother and infant.
Prada Aoyama, Tokyo

What was this?

An Office Tower

This office tower was very typical of its time. It was composed of a metal frame structure to resist the strong Gulf Stream. The structure was stuffed with slabs of regular 4-meter offsets to optimize the surface of the office space. As a result, the profit from rent was maximized. It had a common space on the 20th floor, with a cafeteria and a smoker's terrace above.

Eiffel Tower, Paris

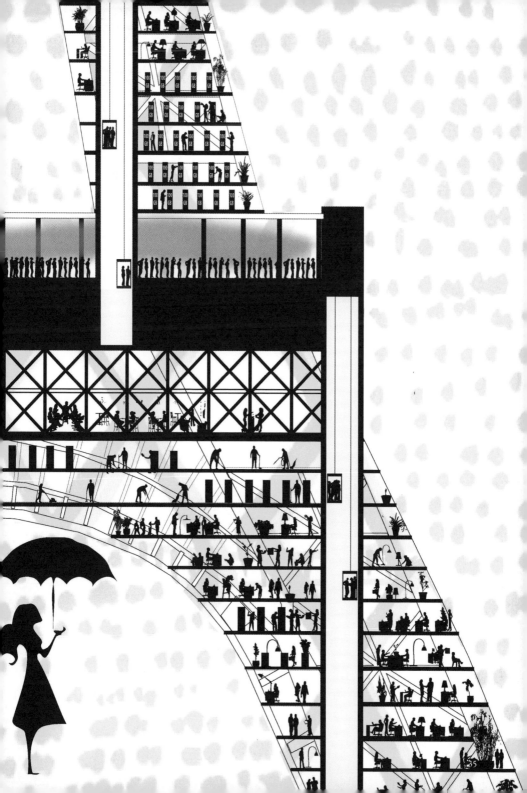

What was this?

A Spaceport

New York City Spaceport was used by 76 spacelines.
The most popular spaceline was NYC – Selene City,
the major settlement on the moon at that time. The
spaceport consisted of 16 gates and could launch
4 shuttles simultaneously. The large number of
passengers per propulsion made it impossible for
the crowd to experience weightlessness. Rumor
had it this structure grew from the bank that
financed space exploration facilities.

Hearst Tower, New York

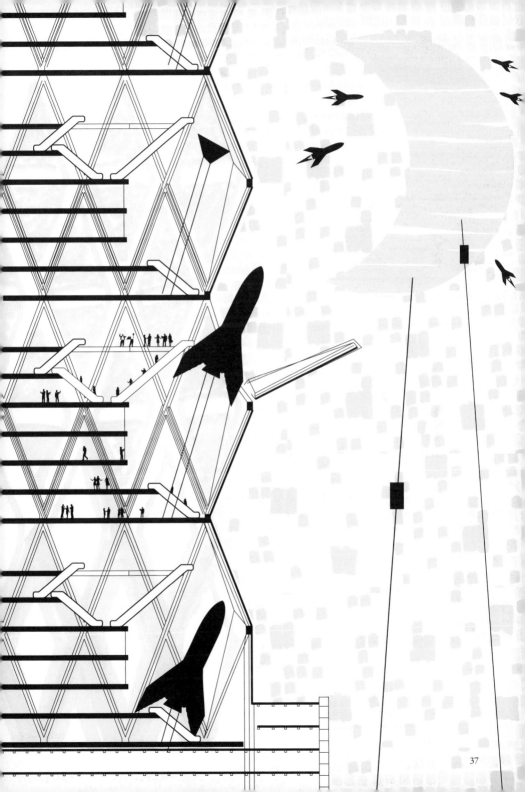

What was this?

A Carwash-Brothel

This explosive mix of architectural programs was a public initiative. The authorities patented this social structure in order to bridle the national population from wild prostitution while offering an efficient vehicle cleaning service as a beautiful alibi for disloyal partners. The center was highly controlled in sanitary and behavioral terms. The prostitutes there were qualified civil servants. The facility became so popular that the cleanness of a car would demonstrate the degree of the owner's adultery.
Phaeno Science Center, Wolfsburg

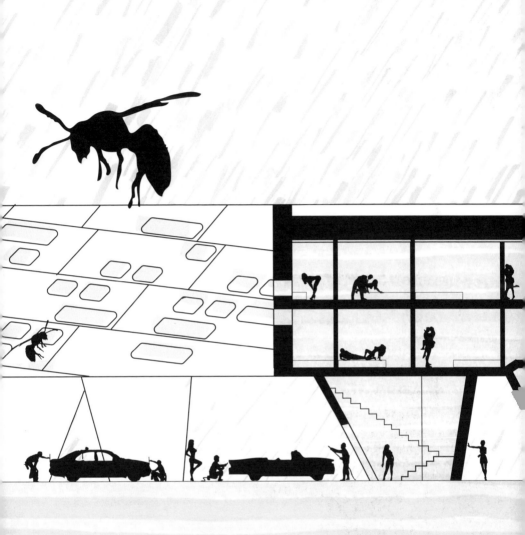

What was this?

A Bunker

The only piece of relic is this pagan drawing, supposedly pure fabulation. There is no evidence to prove this building to be a war bunker. Some historians advocate the proposal that this drawing has been produced by a local nostalgic artist from 2421.
Iberê Camargo Museum, Porto Alegre

What was this?

A Graveyard

Rumors have it that in the early 2000s, people fervently
accepted the notion of Second Life. Some documents
from the 23nd century reported that people in the
early 2000s only had a vague understanding
of Virtuality and Reality. A 23nd century
newspaper caricatured the situation
with this drawing. The following
day it was banned from
publishing in Fourth Life.
International Port
Terminal, Yokohama

What was this?

A Prison

This drawing (2460) found in the Delph Archive speculates on a prison that would have imprisoned those who illegally watched television. This proposition has never been confirmed by scientists who were unable to find LCD-screen traces in the remains after the 2130 flooding. Moreover, it was only soon after the invention of television, which hence might not have been prohibited yet.

Selfridges, Birmingham

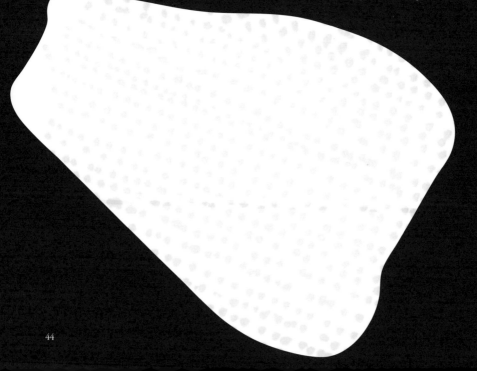

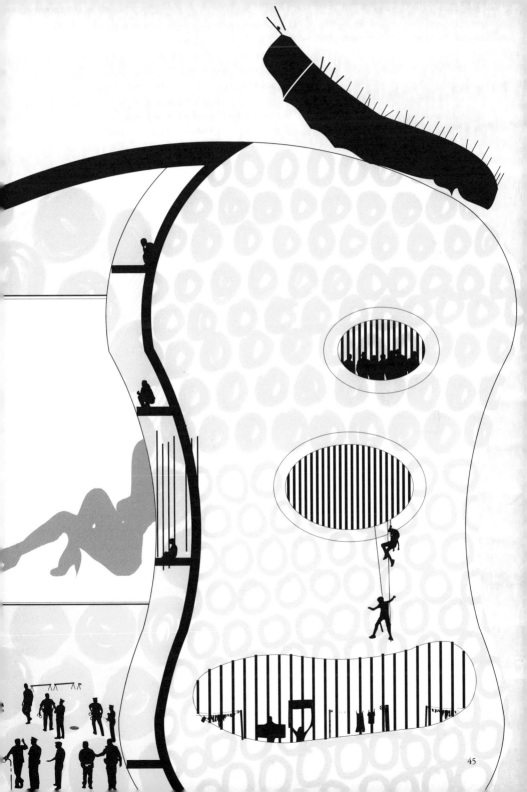

What was this?

A Biomass Energy Plant

Based on existing scientific knowledge, people of the 21st century combined various biowaste and sedimentation techniques in this structure. Perhaps one of the most important inventions of the period, this is believed to be the precursor of the legendary V1.0 Biomass Renewable Energy Machine. With a shape that ensures buoyancy and mobility in case of floods, the invention ultimately failed due to the problem of gathering flies.

Kunsthaus, Graz

What was this?

A Ruin

This former museum has been forsaken, just like the city that it was programmed to save. Bilbao did not survive the numerous economical crises that shortly followed its construction. Titanium, even more than today, was a valuable raw material and its shiny silhouette has been plundered by the villagers for other applications. During this Grey Age, it was trendy to have a coffee table made of one sheet of the structure's titanium cladding.
Guggenheim Museum, Bilbao

What was this?

Sports Park

During the impressive Beijing Olympics Games of the early 2000s, this building was built for Bungee Jump events. That year, the Gold Medal went to a Russian who managed to jump and catch a 1-dollar bill on the ground before bouncing back in the air.

Central Chinese Television Headquarters, Beijing

COMMENTARY ON MONSTERPIECES:
Monsters, frontiers, and interiority

Antoine Picon

In Greek mythology or in fairy tales, monsters usually guard thresholds, boundaries, or frontiers. These thresholds, boundaries, or frontiers can separate inhabited places from forests and deserts, ordinary from enchanted kingdoms, or the domain of the living from the realm of the dead. For Instance, the Sphinx (who was defeated by Oedipus) guarded the entrance to the Greek city of Thebes, while Cerberus was posted at the gate of the underworld. Despite the diversity of the frontiers they watch, monsters do not really care about their exact nature. Their vocation is to threaten and possibly attack those who venture close to it, so that the best prepared, the most motivated, or the very lucky ones only get to pass safely.

While monsters remain strangely indifferent to the nature of the boundary on which they stand, they nevertheless often embody some of its characteristics through exaggerated features or hybridity. With their highly recognizable appearance, monsters are like pictograms conveying the existence of problematic transitions—hence, their interest is both graphic and moral, conveyed in books such as Medieval bestiaries. Even more than the ordinary animals depicted in these books, monsters are highly instructive.

These traditional features of monsters may enable us to understand a little better Aude-Line Duliere and Clara Wong's project. The architectural "monsters" they have gathered in this book mark disconcerting transitions between scales, functions, and uses. Some of these monsters are abnormally large. Rem Koolhaas' CCTV Tower is, for instance, playing with the gigantic. Others challenge received notions about exteriority and interiority, structure or use. Jacques Herzog and Pierre de Meuron's Beijing National Stadium claims to be structurally different from its "Cartesian" predecessors. Elizabeth Diller and Ricardo Scofidio's Blur Building is hard to describe using traditional categories of outside and inside. All of these buildings stand at limits that other architectural realizations usually avoid.

Built monsters are by no means recent. The inclusion of the 1889 Eiffel Tower in the series compiled by Aude-Line and Clara is telling in that respect. But architectural monsters have nevertheless proliferated in the past decades, and this proliferation is even more revealing. It has, of course, to do with globalization and with the increased competitions between cities that all aspire to make a difference using architectural highlights as a beacon of their achievements. From Frank Gehry's Guggenheim Museum in Bilbao to Peter Cook and Colin Fournier's Kunsthaus in Graz, Austria, pretty much all the projects retained by Aude-Line and Clara have to do with urban strategies of distinction.

Among the properties of monsters, one finds, as I mentioned, their recognizable character. Architectural monsters are highly iconic—hence, the seduction they exert on mayors and their advisors who are precisely looking for signs of distinction. In this quest for visibility, function often becomes secondary. Such a trend has, of course, to do with the performalist turn at work in contemporary architecture. Design is more and more akin to a form of action, the efficiency of which is not always dependent on the strict observance of programmatic and functional requirements. Architecture does what it does, and this has not necessarily to do with program and function in the traditional sense, but with a capacity to install oneself in a situation—indeed, to create the situation through one's very presence. Architectural monsters are better understood as built situations than as constructions answering programs and fulfilling functions.

This shift is related to another property of monsters—namely, the fact that they often have a problematic interiority. With their discrepant parts, borrowed from different genres and species, monsters are difficult to understand from an anatomical and physiological standpoint. How is one to make anatomical sense of winged lions? Coupled with the transition from function to iconic performance, this problematic interiority explains the dissociation between envelope and use that characterizes so many of the projects presented in this book. Defining themselves as "rebellious daughters of the Koolhaasian

90s," Aude-Line and Clara's allegedly archaeological reconstructions of possible and often fantastic uses of their monsters may appear as a twisted version of Koolhaas' concept of congestion, as exposed in *Delirious New York*. But it is above all the result of the perplexity generated by the mere sight of monsters, the anatomy of which is always, at best, enigmatic.

In this book, the real rebellion or, rather, departure from the Koolhaasian 90s may have ultimately to do with a totally different perspective from the dystopian denunciation of monsters' transgressions of received boundaries or their indifference towards traditional programmatic and functional expressiveness. No, the real rebellion might have, rather, to do with the implicit rediscovery of a moral gaze upon architectural subjects that contrasts with the cynicism that has been so often associated with Koolhaas' take on the world. By moral I do not mean ethical. These days, with the rise of sustainability concerns and the rediscovery of urban squalor at the scale of global metropolises, we are swamped with ethical propositions regarding architecture and the built environment. Morality is more subjective than ethics; it is felt rather than reasoned at an abstract level. Moral is what one typically finds at the end of a story, to summarize its meaning for the reader. In traditional stories, monsters were always, in an implicit or explicit manner, associated with morality. Their spectacular appearance, their frightening or burlesque demeanor, conveyed lessons about how to live in a world even more fantastic than fiction. The architectural bestiary in this book is ultimately moral insofar that it promotes a certain type of attitude based on a mix of wonder and benign bemusement, something like an architectural wisdom.

COMMENTARY ON MONSTERPIECES:
Yellow Monsters

Monica Ponce de Leon

Monsters are children's friends, in that they are their much-needed enemy. Fright feeds imagination. Fear of that which we cannot understand, fear of lack of control, fear of the yet to come, is channeled into a fascination with scary, fantastic creatures. Exaggeration, deformation, and distortions of the known propel this alternative make-believe world. In childhood these animate figures stand in opposition to the stable disposition of buildings. Children imagine monsters under the bed, but delineate buildings on paper. Home, school, church, playground populate a child's drawings. Eventually, the monster makes an appearance on the frame and wreaks havoc on the scene; children run from playground; monster steps on buildings; house burns under the monster's feet. There is no irony in these pictures, but sometimes a little humor emerges. A little dog barking at the big monster scares the monster. A nod that the monsters are a figment of little imaginations, and nothing to be afraid of. A means of learning how to take control.

Like cartoons, comic strips, or animations, *Monsterpieces* occupies the ground between children's tale and grown-up narrative. Distorting that which we know serves as a lens that amplifies flaws. This calibrated exposure becomes a critique of the subject of our distortion and a commentary on the world around us. Dr. Seuss stories made sense of the postwar era and tackled American demons as well as Geisel's own[1]—white figures empty of color against a tinted background. *The Simpsons'* dysfunctional family makes sense of middle-class contradictions in the post–Cold War era[2]—yellow figures in an otherwise normal world. In their wit, cartoons exert the most powerful form of criticism. Humor draws us in, gives a sense of safety, and leaves us wide open to questions. We trust their good intentions. Parody has been mostly absent from the discipline of architecture, and *Monsterpieces* claims it as a plausible architectural technique. Unstable economic markets, a world at war, and the doom of ecological disaster have, many a time, induced satire. On these occasions, the discipline of architecture has, for the most part, remained unscathed. *Monsterpieces* does not let buildings or their authors get away with it.

Monsters are by definition exceptional, alien to the everyday. They are part of the rule, in that they are the exception. They scare us, in that they prove what we know is unstable. They warn of plausible outcomes, but because they are fantastic, we learn that fright is only temporary, never to be confused with true terror. Monsters play a cathartic role that allows us at once to both escape our fears and confront them. In the Industrial Revolution, Frankenstein's monster surfaced as a man gone awry due to man's making. After two wars, King Kong and Godzilla loomed as threats over our cities. By the 1960s Ultraman came to the rescue against sinister aliens and enormous monsters. A super-humanoid giant from outer space—not a superhero, but more like a monster-hero. In their repurposing, *Monsterpieces* appropriates architectural icons of recent history and magnifies their figures by giving them new use. They stand as alter egos to the excessive originals, bringing into question the golden age of architectural production. To the contemporary eye, familiar with the buildings, these monsters seem to be the original gone awry, a living ruin, a failed experiment. But in the context of economic instability, the excess of the original icons seems to be the real monster. Amid impending ecological degradation, the Yellow Monsters become our monster-heros, implausible alternatives to superbuildings who have seemingly failed to avert disaster. *Monsterpieces'* buildings come to save the day.

[1] An interview with filmmaker Ron Lamothe about his film *The Political Dr. Seuss*. Summarizes Theodore Geisel's work best: "If one had to whittle it down to a few themes and books, I would say they were anti-isolationism/internationalism *(Horton Hears a Who)*, racial equality *(The Sneetches)*, anti-fascism/anti-authoritarianism *(Yertle the Turtle)*, anti-materialism/anti-consumerism *(How the Grinch Stole Christmas and The Lorax)*, environmentalism *(The Lorax)*, and the arms race *(The Butter Battle Book)*." (Wood, Hayley and Ron Lamothe (interview) (August 2004). MassHumanities eNews. Massachusetts Foundation for the Humanities.)

[2] *The Simpsons* as released in 1989, the same year George Bush became president, the year of the collapse of the Berlin Wall, and what has come to be known as the year in which the Cold War ended. The creator, Matt Groening, shaped the family after his own and named the characters after members of his own family.

COMMENTARY ON MONSTERPIECES:
Hyddeous Strength

Jonathan D Solomon

uliere and Wong have written a book that explores the major works of a generation obsessed with architectural form. From the enlightened contemporary perspective of the *now* of social ecology, sustainability, and adaptive urban ecology, their critique is devastating in its application. The purpose of dogmatic shifts such as the one on which this book rests is the rejection of prior models. That Duliere and Wong's book plays this role predictably does not mean that it does not do it well, and should in no way diminish its importance. That it is so pretty in itself doesn't hurt, either. The Form Party, as Sanford Kwinter has called the period from the mid-nineties through the turn of the century, may be over, but the power of forms persists.

Just because a thing is less fashionable doesn't mean we are no longer responsible for it, or its consequences. Buildings can last, as Duliere and Wong remind us, a long time, well past our own tolerance of them. If this book teaches us one thing, it is that the architecture of the pastdecade has not been attentive enough to its own consequences. It has not been self-critical enough. Just look at it!

Is this bestiary merely a compendium of fantastical futures? If you think so, have a look at two besties that have come to life already; the Ryugyong Hotel in Pyongyang, and the Burj Dubai, in what Mike Davis has called the "dreamworld of neoliberalism": Dubai.

How are we meant to understand Burj Dubai on the basis of its form? Surely, it is the Tower of Babel as imagined by Pieter Bruegel the Elder! To accept this would lead us to equate the project with the hubris of Nimrod, to warn that the global practice of architecture teeters on the brink of

Burj Dubai, United Arab Emirates, 2,684 ft, 160 stories. Skidmore, Owings and Merril, Adrian Smith, Architect; Bill Baker, Engineer; Turner Construction Company, Contract Manager. Completion in 2009, pictured 26 March 2008. Photo by Imre Solt.

Ryugyong Hotel, Pyong yang, 1082ft, 105 stories. Baekdu Mountain
Architects & Engineers, architects and contractors. Construction begun
1987, pictured 18 December 2008. Photo by Kernbeiser.

universal language, or to throw up our hands at the impossibilities of transcultural dialogue—in short, to declare the end to progress witnessed in Dubai on the eve of the Burj's completion in early 2009.

Sir David Lyndsay's 1555 reference to the ruins of the tower of Babel, "the shadow of that Hyddeous Strength," ends in an archaic middle-Scots noun that means not power, but its architecture: a castle or a fort. (Readers of C.S. Lewis will recall the use of this reference in that author's 1945 novel, *That Hideous Strength*, from which the title for this text was affectionately borrowed. A devastatingly funny critique of techno-modernism and academic politics can be found within). What does it mean to build for an autocratic, tyrannical regime built on false speculation? Nimrod's architects must have felt a similar thrill for their monsterpiece, and loved their stronghold even when, in ruin, it lay at their feet.

It was certainly springtime for Nimrod in 2008, as work resumed after a 20-year hiatus on Pyongyang's Ryugyong Hotel, under funding from Egyptian communications and construction conglomerate, Orascom. A 1,083-ft. structure begun in 1987 with French funding, the Ryugyong Hotel was abandoned in 1992, and the empty concrete form was left to deteriorate. Seven revolving restaurants were originally planned for the summit of the tower—under the reconfiguration, transmitters for the country's 3G networks went in first, followed by streaks of mirrored glass panels running like landslides down the sheer façade.

Ryugyong is a skyscraper built outside the technological and economic calculus that has governed the typology since its origins in 1890s Chicago. Unoccupied and by all accounts unoccupiable, in a poverty-stricken communist capital, it is incapable of fulfilling Cass Gilbert's 1933 dictum and making the land pay. Rather, in an Orwellian twist, it seems to only accumulate more cost. Incomplete and malevolent in appearance, it is equally incapable of making the land *say*. In fact, the building is commonly masked out of official photographs of the city skyline or alternately pictured as falsely completed on documents such as postage stamps. Dysfunctional as a structure or a symbol, Ryugyong is a true monsterpiece: a radio tower in a nation where radios are outlawed, a façade determined as a product of its own propaganda.

These buildings play victim to sea changes in global political alignment of tyranny, ever lengthening the shadows of that "Hyddeous Strength". In its new glass sheath, the Ryugyong Hotel becomes...a broadcast antenna! Perfect for enabling limited and internal communication amongst an ever more isolated elite, it is cynically clad in the mirror glass of international capitalism. In its new economy, Burj Dubai becomes...a metaphor! The world's biggest one-liner, figuratively and literally. Architects, beware.

Who is responsible for this?

AFTERWORD:
Time, Space, and Monstrosity:
A (Retrospective) User's Guide

Spyros Papapetros

riting the *AFTERWORD* to a book on monsters might be a monstrosity in and of itself. Once all inversions, regressions, and subversions have been verbalized and illustrated, what more is there to add or summarize? One solution might be to fashion this postscript as a monstrous aberration—another coil in the monster's tail. But one might also choose to act methodically: go back, unwind every twist, and break down all of the monster's irregular appendages so that they appear smooth and geometric. Faithful to the ideas of fusion and hybridity pervading all monstrosities, this afterword decides (boldly) to do both: half atlas and half dictionary, half supplement and half (retrospective) user's guide, the afterword both extends and compartmentalizes the central body of the text by bringing into focus its main ideas and/or marginal minutiae. A cluster of adventurous coherences connect each term with the themes orbiting in its periphery, so that these ever-expanding textual associations produce new constellations between architecture, nature, and their parallel histories.

[PRE-]HISTORY The main monstrosities described in this book are temporal in nature. All of the buildings redesigned by the two authors are contemporary, with the notable exception of the Eiffel Tower. In fact, all their recent specimens were completed after 2000, with the exception of Gehry's Guggenheim Museum in Bilbao—the alleged ancestor of all spectacular and iconic buildings of the new millennium. The absence of projects by the Modernist masters is conspicuous. But then again, is not Mies's unrealized 1921 Friedrichstrasse Tower or Le

Corbusier's unbuilt Mundaneum ostensibly reincarnated in several of these contemporary monstrosities? And is not the Eiffel Tower a model for many modern technological hyperboles—a historical origin established both by modern architectural historians like Sigfried Giedion, as well as anti-Modernist critics, such as Jacques Tati? Like the appearance of the Eiffel Tower in Tati's *Playtime* projected on the glass entrance of a Modernist building and representing both a bygone origin and a reflection of architecture's modern-day predicament, so do several of the contemporary monsters of this volume assume the role of a new origin, which is impossible to fix in time and space.

Following the "post-Koolhaasian" logic of Aude-Line Duliere and Clara Wong, their book is a "retrospective manifesto" for contemporary architecture; its complex understanding of socio-temporal space is based on a "retroperspective"—an **INVERTED PERSPECTIVE** reminiscent of Medieval paintings, in which the front side of the object (building or furniture) appears smaller, while its rear surfaces are magnified.

"What *was* that?" ask Duliere and Wong when referring to a building, instead of inquiring what "that" *is* or what it *will be*? Their descriptions refer to a distant future in which the function of each building is entirely reconfigured. And yet while moving towards the future, the buildings reappear as relics of a (pre)historical condition. The entire narrative is written in the mode of a "future anterior"—a psychological representation of time in which objects are re-projected into the future as what they *will have been*. The large sea mammals floating on the margins of built structures or the gigantic insects creeping on the buildings' skins are the organic signs of a **PRE/POST/EROUS** history of architecture: a history oscillating between the overwhelming fauna of prehistory and the murky waters of *post-histoire*.

The event that allows the hybridization of temporalities and the reciprocity between *pre* and *post* is the (virtual) occurrence of an **APOCALYPSE**. A certain cataclysmic event (that has happened or is about to occur) appears as the retrospective cause for the ruinous condition that some of the formerly resplendent buildings have fallen. Often, monsters would be considered as omens of an imminent deluge—a cosmic catastrophe that would befall mankind and force it to start again from the beginning.[1] Apocalypse creates a desert—a seemingly infinite terrain devoid of buildings, yet replete with architectural possibilities. Having persisted through a deluge, the buildings reappear as post-apocalyptic survivors. They have more of an **AFTERLIFE** than a real life. Some of them, like the "cloud" pavilion by Diller+Scofidio, had only a very brief life. Yet it is this very transience that makes the legacy of such architectural vampires live forever.

[1] Aby Warburg, "Pagan-Antique Prophecy in Words and Images in the Age of Luther" (1920) in *The Renewal of Pagan Antiquity*, edited by Kurt Forster and translated by David Britt (Santa Monica: The Getty Research Institute, 1999), 597-697.

HISTORIOGRAPHY In this post-apocalyptic scenario, the buildings are archaeologically recovered by a projective historiography. Even though built, each of the projects transforms into an experimental model designed to test a number of alternative hypotheses. There is a monstrous element in this speculative history that raises what Timothy Hyde describes in the preface as the act of prophecy or historical ***PROGNOSTICATION*** to the level of a post-historical event. In his reflections on "the history of the immediate future," Reyner Banham envisioned the historian as a computer analyst, inserting all hard data from past histories and modern-day science to obtain a "graph" of future architectural developments.[2] But what if instead of these hard scientific data or major historical developments, one feeds the historiographical machine with all the marginal aberrations of both architectural history (what Walter Benjamin would call "the detritus of history"[3]) as well as all the monstrous accidents of natural science? What kind of hyperbolic graph would the architectural historian's computer then produce? This parabolic graph is the composite diagram produced by the two authors' graphic manipulations of recent building data in this volume. Unlike Banham, Duliere and Wong invert the present with the future to construct a history of the *immediate past*.

MUSEUM The graphic project of the two authors bridges the gaps between book, exhibition, and museum. Their illustrated anthology reads like an exhibition catalog surveying the (natural) history of contemporary architecture. The book presents a ***NATURAL HISTORY*** museum replete with fossils, bones, animals, and antediluvian monsters. While submerged in prehistory, the same project is also a "**grand tour**" of recent global architecture graphically reinvented in the pages of the textual museum. What is illustrated is not only a collection of building samples, but a series of (natural) processes for the transmogrification of buildings in terms of function, organization, ambience, and skin—the new "four elements of architecture."

[POST] FUNCTION In the graphic manipulations by Duliere and Wong, the skin and external form of each building remain essentially the same, while their interior structure is fundamentally altered. In certain cases, the skeleton almost disappears, creating an interiorized desert where, as Antoine Picon observes, any function, program, or activity can take place. The assignment of a new function in each of these converted spaces is heuristic. The former office tower, department store, library, stadium, cultural center or museum become beach, greenhouse, swimming pool, car wash, ruin, but also office tower, prison, and—again—museum. Some functions perish and some survive, yet in an entirely different building envelope. Ultimately, function appears as an ornament, a rhetorical flourish added onto the existing structure that accentuates the building's programmatic indeterminacy. Monstrosity, then, is no longer in the

[2] Reyner Banham, "The History of the Immediate Future," *RIBA Journal* 68 (May 1961), 252-260, 269.
[3] Walter Benjamin, "Painting, Jugendstil, Novelty" in *The Arcades Project*, translated by Howard Eiland and Kevin McLaughlin; prepared on the basis of the German volume edited by Rolf Tiedemann. (Cambridge, Mass: Harvard University Press, 1999), 545.

external morphology, the overt or introverted zoomorphism of the building structure, but in the ambient **hybridization of functions**—the implementation of alternative uses in an organism originally programmed for a different performance.

Architectural historians argue that the Modernist reinvention of the concept of function in architecture coincides with late 18th century developments in natural science: in particular organic anatomy and the invention of biology. But all functional analogies that we see, for example, in the "organic" architectural theory of Lodoli are based on the model of a unified organism with separate functions, yet a central mode or organization.[4] One may only wonder what type of ***POST-ORGANIC*** analogies one could make with architecture based on the pre-Classical epistemes of monsters: creatures with a radically inhomogeneous organic structure that has no central core of organization, but is suffused by peripheral extensions and (de)tails.

IMAGE While function ostensibly disappears or is reduced to an all-encompassing "ruin," image triumphantly survives in the building monsters of 2000. The only stable property of these transforming architectures is their exteriorized iconicity crystallized in their contour, texture, and/or shape. Each of the monsters in this volume is reduced to a single outline—an eidetic prototype—emptied of content, yet particularly memorable as a two-dimensional gestalt. All of the iconic monsterpieces of 2000—most of them highly "sculptural"—regress to what Giedion would call the **"first conception of space"**: a state in which the building functions as a mere volume (made up of an assemblage of flat and permanent planes)—such as, for example, the Egyptian pyramid. Such sculptural buildings "radiate space outwards," writes Giedion, but have almost no interior.[5] Like the Pirelli Tower in Milan or the Empire State Building in New York (among an endless series of similarly iconic modern skyscrapers), the building functions as an image—a sculptural or pictorial monolith. Image is the new function—the pictorial expression of social investment on the building's surface.

SCALE[LESS] Some of the projects featured in this book appear to have no scale; they could be overwhelmingly large or infinitely small. While they may be gigantic in size, they can be reduced to a miniscule shape, such as an egg, a donut, a condom, or an amoeba. The exploded dogs, frogs, rabbits, whales, and other animals inhabiting the milieu of these buildings make the incommensurability of scale even more apparent. Monstrosity, then, exists in the protean quality to usurp scale and traverse cosmic faculties from the micro to the macro level. Decisive proof for the hybridity of scale is provided in the interior cover of this book, in which we see all building models densely packed and flattened into a pattern, reminiscent of the wallpaper and

---

[4] Adrian Forty, "Function" in *Words and Buildings: A Vocabulary of Modern Architecture* (New York: Thames and Hudson, 2000), 174-195.

[5] Sigfried Giedion, "Introduction—The three space conceptions in architecture" in *Architecture and the Phenomena of Transition*, (Cambridge, Mass: Harvard University Press, 1971), 1-6.

fabric designs by the Eames in the 1950s. Like the cosmic designs of the Eames, the building motifs floating in the interior fabric of this volume resemble either microscopic biological patterns (blood cells or skin tissue), or planetary bodies of a densely populated galaxy.

[POLY]FORM Monsters are fashioned as exceptions—permanent deviations from all physiological or aesthetic norms. Yet even within this exceptional state, there are certain principles or laws that all monsters stringently adhere to. One of these is the law of *HYBRIDITY*—the mixed, inhomogeneous nature of the monster that fuses limbs, organs, or organic functions from a variety of animal categories. Animal-headed men (such as the gods of Egyptian religion), women with a bulbous vegetal head (such as the popular mythological figure of Mandragora), or men with wings or tails (fantastic remnants of former evolutionary states) growing from their spine: the proportional analogy between the human, the animal, or the vegetal is never a one-to-one ratio in any monster. There is an intricate asymmetrical law of composition in the bodily architecture of the teratomorphous creature. Monstrosity, then, is not a matter of great dimensions, but of incommensurable proportions between the several parts of the building organism. Following Wittkower, if Renaissance and Classical architecture rely on a system of ideal anthropomorphic *PROPORTION*, what are the architectures that could be created according to the principles of teratomorphism? The teratomorphic model is built upon a more intricate notion of analogy and proportion than anthropomorphism. It encompasses relations not between body parts of a single (overprivileged) creature, but between a variety of animal forms and functions across scales.

COMPOSITION The main characteristic of monsters is, thus, the *composite* element of their representation—the way their bodies combine elements from a variety of organisms to create a model that appears unique, yet reminiscent of a variety of preexisting models. Such complex composition is reminiscent of Freud's description of the "composite figures" that we see in dreams. No human figure is of one person; like Francis Galton's criminological portraits made by the superimposition of four, five, or even seven portraits of convicted criminals, every face we envision has the beard, nose, ears, forehead, or chin of a different person.[6] Instead of a definite "ideal" type, what we end up seeing is the blurry image of an animated outline—a transparent contour whose multiple edges appear to vibrate. One might be tempted to (psycho)analyze several of the building monsterpieces presented in this volume in terms of their composite background—the way that each of these architectures quotes, recycles, and superimposes several historical models. While most of these buildings—such as Jean Nouvel's

[6] Sigmund Freud, "The Interpretation of Dreams," *The Standard Edition of the Complete Psychological Works of Sigmund*, translated and edited by J. Strachey (London: Hogarth Press, 1953) Vol. IV, 293.
[7] Reyner Banham, "Critcism: Pirelli Building, Milan, Ponti, Nervi and Associates, Architects," *Architectural Review* 129 (March 1961), 194-200.
[8] Warburg, *The Renewal of Pagan Antiquity*, 639.

Torre Agbar or even Herzog and de Meuron's Beijing National Stadium—have what Banham described (in reference to Ponti's Pirelli Tower) as a decisively "closed form," they open up to a variety of precedents.[7] Monstrosity, then, yields uniqueness, yet is recreated by a host of partial repetitions.

MULTI-HEAD/MULTI-LEG   Monsters often have many heads (like the Herculean Hydra) or many legs (like the wild pigs with eight feet—four of them growing upwards from their spine—shown in engravings from the period of German Reformation).[8] The *polychephalic* creature (reminiscent of the Freudian unconscious described by Lacan as a "crowd of characters" with many heads but no faces) is the epitome of diffused association.[9] A polycephalic architectural organism would be one of multiple centers, but with no central point or axis of organization (again, like the Freudian unconscious, the architectural organism becomes essentially *acephalic*). On the other hand, multi-legged animals—such as insects or amoebae (with multiple pseudopodia)—present the model of an organism whose entire sensory or motor mechanism is eccentrically focused on the organism's bodily periphery. The entire animal or building subsists on its extensions—the bodily appendages that undermine its core. One is reminded of the giant **INSECTS** infesting several of the buildings of this volume: bees, termites, and other multi-legged creepers, reminiscent perhaps of Le Corbusier's fascination with the work of entomologists like Fabre. In his unpublished manuscript on *Magical Architecture*, Frederick Kiesler described the architecture of termites as an ecologically sound form of building made not through the superfluous addition, but by the extraction of building matter from the ground.[10] The architecture created by the termites of this volume refers to a historical rather than a material extraction, which nevertheless can also serve as building material.

HYPERTROPHY   In its multiplication of heads, legs, and arms, monstrosity is a condition where the hypertrophy and multiplication of a limb causes that organ to become obsolete. Is there a parallel to be drawn with contemporary architecture? Can the very hypertrophy of technological appendages prosthetically attached (or spontaneously grown) by modern building organisms also lead to functional obsolescence? From Archigram's machine-like tentacles of the 1960s to the mechanical entrails displayed on the façade of Beaubourg, technology organically grows from the enhanced architectural organism not as an internal network or function, but as a system of semi-autonomous appendages (party functional and partly cosmetic) that have the tendency to detach themselves from the external envelope or skin.

[9] Jacques Lacan, *The Seminar of Jacques Lacan. Book II: The ego in Freud's theory and in the technique of psychoanalysis, 1954-55*, edited by Jacques-Alain Miller, translated by S. Tomaselli (New York: Norton, 1991), 167.

[10] Frederick Kiesler, "Magic Architecture" in *Friedrich Kiesler: Endless House 1947-1961* (Vienna: Hatje Cantz Publishers, 2003).

AQUEOUS ENVIRONMENT And why is there so much water in several of these monster buildings? The swimming pool, the beach, the aquarium, or even the car wash are filled, surrounded by, or operate with water. Even the "cloud" building by D+S is transferred from its original location on a lake in Switzerland to the port of New York. Transference, submersion, and liquidity are again the formal processes of the unconscious—the repository of repressed desires in which solidity becomes obsolete. Yet here, water signifies a regression not only to psychological space, but also to the space of prehistory and our antediluvian amphibian existence, when water was the singular milieu and all living beings were sea polyps (Sergei Eisenstein describes the formal memory traces of this "protoplasmatic" condition in his incomplete essay on Disney).[11] The water floating in the illustrations of this volume also proves that the "aqueous humor" of architecture is not a singular element of Le Corbusier's buildings or his urbanism (as Robert Slutszky would suggest), but also a larger property of modern and contemporary architecture.[12]

Water also signifies a space of memory, as well as ecological or environmental erosion. As the authors acknowledge, the book advocates a different form of *SUSTAINABILITY*—an ecological strategy relying not on the preservation of resources, but on hybridity, erosion, expenditure, and, ultimately, decay. Within the normative discourse about sustainability in architecture that, too, might be a fresh, even if monstrous, perspective.

ANALOGY Water is also the environment of infinite association—a space allowing multiple forms of analogical relation. Every correspondence between buildings and animal forms demonstrated in this volume discloses the work of analogy. Analogy establishes forms of intimacy between natural specimens and man-made objects which might otherwise appear distant. In that they combine components from a variety of animal species, monsters are analogies in themselves. Their analogies with building, therefore, are analogies of the second degree. The architectural monstrosities described in this book are, then, the fossils of an ancient analogical mentality (which, for Foucault, vanishes with the advent of classical episteme).[13] Architectural analogies affirm relations between objects instead of continuously rejecting them; they say "yes" instead of "no" by breaking down architectural partitions.[14]

Based on such analogical relations, this book celebrates the art of optical similitude—the "this *looks* like that" mentality—which restores the value of visual *RESEMBLANCE*. If the CCTV Tower looks like "big underpants" or the Beijing National Stadium like a "bird's nest," it does not mean that they *are* either underpants or nest. And yet both the nest and the

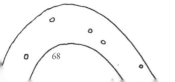

11 Sergei Eisenstein, *Eisenstein on Disney* , edited by Jay Leda and translated by A. Upchurch, (London: Methuen, 1988).
12 Robert Slutzky, "Aqueous Humor" in *Oppositions*, no. 19/20 (Winter/Spring 1980), 28-51.

underpants analogies become forms of communication for grasping the incommensurability and fundamentally incommunicative character of these two buildings. Allegory, absurdity, irony, and metaphor are the new forms of teratological analogy.

WONDER The widespread analogies criss-crossing this anthology of contemporary architectural monsters make it appear as a Medieval "book of wonders"—a collection of fables in which one miraculous event follows another, with no interpretation in between. The reader marvels at the sequence of wonders and feels no need to explain anything. This is why it is impossible to write a critical conclusion at the end of this book. The author of the afterword can only capitulate to the logic of the fable. The "rebellious daughters of the Koolhaasian 90s" can continue to create new monsters based on delirious association and impeccably designed conceit. Monster after monster, image after image, monstrosity turns into a sumptuously orchestrated sequence of architectural myths with no critical attempt toward interpretation. Post-criticality is, after all, another monster of the 90s, but at least here it is supported by irony, wit, and sheer brilliance, and does not mask itself as a "pragmatist," or "objective" mode of architecture.

EDUCATION Finally, since every children's book has to end with a didactic conclusion, a word about education. Doing some market research on contemporary children's books (especially of the preschool level), one might be surprised to discover how many of them are about monsters. It may well be that such picture books predominantly portray benevolent or harmless giants that do not frighten children (which might be an even greater monstrosity, since such books strive to transform monsters to normal creatures that are uncannily similar to humans). But why give children any books about monsters at all? Far from making ethical statements for the appropriateness of monster books for juveniles, the profusion of such literature discloses the affinity that exists between the hybrid character of teratomorphous creatures and the nascent bodily and mental condition of human beings that are not yet fully formed. Monsters are supposedly malformed or overformed, while children are ostensibly underformed, yet both creatures share the possibility of extensive transformation. Both the monster and the child live in a world of infinite potential. Like tadpoles, they belong into the world, yet their bodily appendages are in a pregnant state of anticipation. In this ostensible lack of form, program, or function lies the ultimate analogy with contemporary architecture.

Ultimately, the monster is an educational model—an edifying mechanism (a function that is perhaps close to what Antoine Picon describes as the "moral" character of monster stories).

---

[13] Michel Foucault "The Four Similitudes (The Prose of the World)" in *The Order of Things: An Archaeology of the Human Sciences* (c1970) (London: Routledge, 1986), 17-25.
[14] Geoffrey E R Lloyd, *Polarity and Analogy: Two Types of Argumentation in Early Greek Thought* (London: Cambridge University Press, 1966).

It represents not learning but **UN-LEARNING**—an apparatus not for reaffirming, but for escaping established norms. What would the consequences of this monstrous education be for architecture neophytes? If the entire trajectory of Postmodern architecture is informed by "learning (or un-learning) from Las Vegas" (a fabulous monster city of the American desert), what are the educational benefits of learning from the individual monsterpieces of 2000— equally mythical, yet unexplored in their new iterations of "ducks" and "decorated sheds"?

REGRESSIVE EVOLUTION   And a final postscript that circles back to the temporal vicissitudes of architectural monstrosities. Discourses about monsters have resurfaced in several periods of architecture—from the Gothic to Baroque and Rococo, and during the last century from Art Nouveau and Surrealism, to Postmodernism and Deconstruction. So why a book on architectural monsters at the close of the first decade of the new millennium?[15] Would such a seemingly atavistic turn imply progress, regression, or an entirely different state of transformation? Towards the turn of the previous century, a group of Belgian natural theorists and sociologists published a book on the idea of "regressive evolution"—a supplement to, as well as sociopolitical critique of, Darwin's earlier theories. According to the Belgian scientists, every (r)evolution is preceded by a form of devolution. No progress can ever occur without regression; no forward movement can take place without recoil. In order to gain one thing, an organism has to lose something else.[16] Atrophy and degeneration were essential processes for the continuation of life, and so were organic rudiments and relics. Could discourses about monstrosity in architecture, then, have a similarly vital organic function? Could the very transformation of contemporary buildings into relics or rudiments of their former function, in fact, propel their evolution in architectural discourse? And would the curious monsters exhibited in this volume therefore promote the animal survival of contemporary architecture within a fundamentally altered ecological or technological milieu? Versus the linear progress of Renaissance and Classical architectural discourses or the radical discontinuity of historical process espoused by the modern movement, recent architectural culture advances another model of history—that of regression, temporal revolution, and spiraling anachronism. By turning back or *looking back* at itself from a distance, contemporary architecture reinstates its critical dimension through a series of miraculously inventive and playfully ironic historiographical operations. And that might be the most prescient form of monstrosity retrospectively manifested in this splendidly illustrated volume.

[15] Anthony Vidler, "Planets, Comets, Dinosaurs (and Bugs): Prehistoric Subjects / Posthistoric Identities" in *Warped Space* (Cambridge, Mass: The MIT Press, 2000), 243-257.

[16] Jean Demoor, Jean Massart, and Émile Vandervelde, *L'évolution régressive en biologie et sociologie* (Paris: Alcan, 1897). English edition: *Evolution by Atrophy in Biology and Sociology*, translated by Chalmers Mitchell (New York: International Scientific Series, D. Appleton and Company, 1899).

APPENDIX:
Bibliography and filmography

Bibliography

Abbot, Edwin A. *Flatland: A Romance of Many Dimensions.* London: Seeley, 1884.

Aberdeen Bestiary, Univ. Lib. MS 24, Aberdeen University Library, 12th century.

Allen, Stanley, Ben van Berkel, Caroline Bos, Robert E. Somol, Peter Eisenman, Manuel De Landa, Christine Buci-Glucksman, Andrew E. Benjamin, Karl S. Chu, Brian Massumi, Greg Lynn, Mark Rakatansky, and Sanford Kwinter. "Diagram Work." *Any* 23 (1998): 14–62.

Aranda, Benjamin, Chris Lasch, Cecil Balmont (Foreword) and Sanford Kwinter (Afterword). *Pamphlet Architecture 27:* "Tooling." New York: Princeton Architectural Press, 2005.

Ballard, J. G. *The Drowned World.* London: Indigo, 1997.

Blanciak, Francois. *Siteless: 1001 Building Forms.* Cambridge, MA: MIT Press, 2008.

Cook, Peter. *Archigram* (all issues, 1972).

Desprez, Francois. *Les Songes Drolatiques de Pantagruel ou sont contenues plusieurs figures de l'invention de maistre François Rabelais: & dernière oeuvre d'iceluy, pour la récréation des bons esprits.* Paris: Richard Breton, 1565.

Desprez, Francois. *Recueil de la diversité des habits, qui sont de present en usage, tant es pays d'Europe, Asie, Affrique & Isles sauvages, le tout fait apres le naturel.* Paris: Richard Breton, 1564.

Di Palma, Vittiria, Diana Periton, Marina Lathouri, *Intimate Metropolis: Urban Subject in the Modern City.* New York: Routledge, 2008.

Dunster, David, Stefan Benisch, Toyo Ito, Peter Ahrends, Donald L. Bates, Antoine Predock, Michael H.Russum, Peter L. Wilson, Matthias Sauerbruch, Massimiliano Fuksas, Kisho Kurokawa, Peter Wislocki, Zoltan E. Pali, Stanley Tigerman, Vittorio Gregotti, Alberto Campo Baeza, John Miller, Ken Yeang, Farshid Moussavi, Alejandro Zaera Polo, Lawrence Nield, John Ronan, Fumihiko Maki, and Tshumi Bernard. "Design Essence [The Diagram]." *Architectural Review 129,1307* (2006): 28–74.

Durand, Jean-Nicolas-Louis. *Recueil et parallèle des édifices de tout genre, anciens et modernes: remarquables par leur beauté, par leur grandeur ou par leur singularité, et dessinés sur une meme échelle.* Paris: Ecole Polytechnique, 1800.

Foucault, Michel. *The Order of Things: An Archaeology of the Human Sciences.* New York: Pantheon Books, 1971.

Frascari, Marco. *Monsters of Architecture: Anthropomorphism in Architectural Theory*. Lanham, MD: Rowman & Littlefield Publishing, 1991.

Friedman, Yona. *Cartoon-Manuals (in) Pro Domo*. Barcelona: Actar, 2006.

Fuller, Buckminster. *Tetrascroll: Godilocks and the Three Bears, A Cosmic Fairy Tale*. New York: St Martins Press, 1982.

Gesner, Conrad. *Historae Animalium*. Zurich: 1551–1558.

Gould, Stephen Jay. *The Flamingo's Smile: Reflections in Natural History*. New York: Norton, 1985.

Guberman, Marc, Jacob Reidel, and Frida Rosenberg. *Perspecta 40 "Monster."* Cambridge, MA: MIT Press, 2008.

Ito, Toyo. "Diagrams Architecture." *El Croquis 19* (1998).

Joyce, James. *Ulysses*. Paris: Shakespeare and Company, 1922.

Juster, Norton. *The Dot and the Line: A Romance Comic in Lower Mathematics*. New York: 1963.

Koolhaas, Rem. "Byzantium Project," in *S, M, L, XL*. New York: Monacelli Press, 1995.

Koolhaas, Rem. *Post-Occupancy*. Milan: Editorial Domus, 2006.

La Fontaine, Jean de. *Fables choisies, mises en vers/par M. de la Fontaine*. Paris: Chez Claude Barbin, au Palais sur le Perron de la sainte Chapelle, 1668.

Lissitzky, El. *About Two Squares*. Berlin: Scythian Press, 1922.

Lykosthenes, Konrad, *Prodigiorum ac ostentorum chronicon, quae praeter naturae ordinem motum, et operationem, et in superioribus & his inferioribus mundi regionibus ab exordio mundi usque ad haec nostra tempora, acciderunt*. Basiliae: Per Henricum Petri, 1557.

Macaulay, David. *Motel of the Mysteries*. Boston Houghton Mifflin, 1979.

Mostafavi, Mohsen and David Leatherbarrow. *On Weathering: The Life of Buildings in Time*. Cambridge, MA: MIT Press, 1993.

Moussavi, Farshid and Michael Kubo. *The Function of Ornament*. Barcelona: Actar, 2006.

Ourednik, Patrik. *Europeana: A Brief History of the Twentieth Century*. Normal: Dalkey Archive Press, 2005.

Paré Ambroise. *Des monstres et prodiges*. Paris: G. Buon, 1585.

Punday, Daniel. "Narrative Performance in the Contemporary Monster Story." *The Modern Language Review 97,4* (2002): 803t–820.

Railing, Patricia. *More About wo Squares*. Cambridge, MA: MIT Press, 1991.

Riley, Terence. *The Changing of the Avant-Garde: Visionary Architectural Drawing from the Howard Gilman Collection*. New York: The Museum of Modern Art, 2002.

Rochester Bestiary, British Library, Royal MS 12 F. xiii, England, 1230.

Scott, Felicity D. *Living Archive 7: Ant Farm*. Barcelona: Actar, 2008.

Sendak, Maurice. *Where the Wild Things Are*. New York: Harper & Row, 1963.

Somol, Robert.E. "12 Reasons to Get Back Into Shape." In *Content*, edited by Rem Koolhaas. Köln: Taschen, 2004.t

Somol, Robert.E. "Dummy ext, or the Diagrammatic Basic of Contemporary Architecture." In *Diagram Diaries*, Peter Eisenman. New York: Universe, 1999.

Toulouse-Lautrec, Henri de. *A Bestiary*. Cambridge, MA: Fogg Art Museum and the Harvard College Library, 1970.

Vidler, Anthony. "Diagrams of Diagrams: Architectural Abstraction and Modern Representation." *Representations 72* (2000): 1–20.

Vidler, Anthony. "Diagrammi di Utopia = Diagrams of Utopia." *Lotus International 123* (2004): 28–41.

Witte, Ron. "Go Figure." *Log 5*, (2005): 76–81

Zaera-Polo, Alejandro. "The Hokusai Wave." *Perspecta 37* (2005): 78–85.

Filmography

Alphaville, une étrange aventure de Lemmy Caution. Dir. Jean-Luc Godard, Athos Films. 1965.

Blade Runner. Dir. Ridley Scott, The Ladd Company. 1982.

Children of Men. Dir. Alfonso Cuarón, Universal Pictures. 2006.

Fahrenheit 451. Dir. François Truffaut, Anglo Enterprises. 1966.

Gattaca. Dir. Andrew Niccol, Columbia Pictures Corporation. 1997.

La Jetée. Dir. Chris Marker, Argos Films. 1962.

The Matrix. Dir. Andy Wachowski and Larry Wachowski, Groucho II Film Partnership. 1999.

Twelve Monkeys. Dir. Terry Gilliam, Universal Pictures. 1995.

List of Illustrations

Page 13: Courtesy of Bibliothèque Municipale de Tours. by ©BM de Tours (Bibliothèque Municipale de Tours), Rés. 3540.

Page 14: Courtesy of the "Bibliothèque Interuniversitaire de Médecine" © BIUM (Paris), Cote BIUM : 1709.

Page 16: Courtesy of the Museum Meermanno-Westreenianum.

Page 21, 23, 25, 27, 29, 31, 33, 35, 37, 39, 41, 43, 45, 47, 49, 51: vector drawings of people, animals, plants, and fixtures ©iStockphoto.com. downloaded from www.istockphoto.com using our membership.

Page 59: Courtesy of the photographer, Imre Solt.

Page 60: Courtesy of the photographer, Kernbeiser.

Building Credits

Plate I	Jean Nouvel, *Torre Agbar*, office building, 2005. Barcelona, Spain. *Page 20*
Plate II	OMA, Rem Koolhaas, *Casa da Música*, concert hall, 2005. Porto, Portugal. *Page 22*
Plate III	Jacques Herzog and Pierre de Meuron, *Beijing National Stadium*, 2008. Beijing, China. *Page 24*
Plate IV	Elizabeth Diller and Ricardo Scofidio, *Blur Building*, Exposition Pavilion for Swiss Expo, 2002. Yverdon-les-bains, Switzerland. *Page 26*
Plate V	OMA, Rem Koolhaas, *Seattle Central Library*, 2004. Seattle, Washington, U.S. *Page 28*
Plate VI	Will Alsop, *Sharp Centre for Design*, Ontario College of Art & Design, 2004. Toronto, Canada. *Page 30*
Plate VII	Jacques Herzog and Pierre de Meuron, *Prada Store*, 2003. Tokyo, Japan. *Page 32*
Plate VIII	Gustave Eiffel, *Eiffel Tower*, entrance arch for the 1889 World's Fair. Paris, France. *Page 34*
Plate IX	Norman Foster, *Hearst Tower*, office building, 2006. New York, U.S. *Page 36*
Plate X	Zaha Hadid, *Phaeno Science Center*, 2005. Wolfsburg, Germany. *Page 38*
Plate XI	Alvaro Siza Vieira, *Ibêre Camargo Museum*, Ontario College of Art & Design, 2008. Porto Alegre, Brazil. *Page 40*
Plate XII	Foreign Office Architects, Farshid Moussavi, and Alejandro Zaera-Polo, *Yokohama International Port Terminal*, 2002. Yokohama, Japan. *Page 42*
Plate XIII	Future Systems, Jan Kaplicky, and Amanda Levete, *Selfridges*, department store, 2002. Birmingham, UK. *Page 44*
Plate XIV	Peter Cook and Colin Fournier, *Kunsthaus*, art museum celebrating the European Capital of Culture, 2003. Graz, Austria. *Page 46*
Plate XV	Frank Gehry, *Guggenheim Museum Bilbao*, art museum, 1997. Bilbao, Spain. *Page 48*
Plate XVI	OMA, Rem Koolhaas, *CCTV*, headquarters, 2002. Beijing, China. *Page 50*

Authors and Contributors

Aude-Line Duliere and **Clara Wong** are rebellious daughters of the Koolhaasian 90s. They hold Master of Architecture degrees from Harvard Graduate School of Design, and together are a model of active global collaboration. **Aude-Line Duliere** is an architect and movie production designer assistant in the U.S. and across Europe, with a Bachelor of Architecture degree *cum laude* from the Institut Superieur d'Architecture La Cambre and a Master's degree from Sint-Lucas Architectuur Brussels. Her academic work builds on the dual nature of her experience and explores the crossroads between architecture and cinema. **Clara Wong** is a practicing architect, artist, and part-time assistant professor at the University of Hong Kong, with academic activities spanning both the U.S. and Hong Kong. She received her Bachelor's degree *summa cum laude* from Princeton University School of Architecture, and graduated with accolades from the Princeton University Program in Visual Arts, focusing on Drawing and Painting.

Stan Allen
Dean and Professor, School of Architecture, Princeton University
Stan Allen has been Dean of Princeton University School of Architecture since 2002, after 13 years at Columbia University, where he was director of the Advanced Design Program at the Graduate School of Architecture. He heads the firm Stan Allen Architect in Brooklyn, NY, which has recently completed houses in New York and Los Angeles, and has won numerous landscape and architecture competitions. Responding to the complexity of the modern city in creative ways, Stan Allen has developed an extensive catalog of urban strategies—in particular, looking at field theory, landscape architecture, and ecology as models to revitalize the practices of urban design.

Timothy W. Hyde
Assistant Professor, Harvard University Graduate School of Design, Department of Architecture

Timothy Hyde is Assistant Professor of Architecture at the Harvard University Graduate School of Design. He is a historian of 20th century architecture and architectural theory.

Ralph A. Lerner
Dean, Faculty of Architecture, The University of Hong Kong

Ralph Lerner is Dean of the Faculty of Architecture at The University of Hong Kong, following his position of Dean and George Dutton Professor of Architecture at Princeton University School of Architecture. He held academic positions at Harvard University Graduate School of Design, the Polytechnic of Central London, and the University of Virginia School of Architecture. He currently serves as the American Institute of Architects International Director. He has been in professional practice in Hong Kong, the United States, and England for 25 years and heads the firm of Ralph Lerner Architect PC in Princeton, New Jersey.

Mohsen Mostafavi
Dean, Alexander and Victoria Wiley Professor of Design, Harvard University Graduate School of Design

Prior to the GSD, Mohsen Mostafavi was Dean at the College of Architecture at Cornell University, and the Chairman of the London Architectural Association School of Architecture. He serves on the jury of the Holcim Foundation for Sustainable Construction, has served on the design committee of the London Development Agency and the RIBA Gold Medal, and is involved as a consultant on many international architectural and urban projects. An architect and educator, he has authored seminal books and essays, including *On Weathering: The Life of Buildings in Time* (with David Leatherbarrow, MIT), *Structure As Space, and Landscape Urbanism: A Manual for the Machinic Landscape* (AA Publications).

Spyros Papapetros
Assistant Professor, History and Theory, Princeton University, School of Architecture

Spyros Papapetros is an assistant professor at the School of Architecture and a member of the Media and Modernity Program at Princeton University. His work focuses on the intersections between architecture and the visual arts, as well as psychoanalysis, historiography, and aesthetics.

Antoine Picon

Professor, Department of Architecture, Harvard University Graduate School of Design

Antoine Picon is Professor of the History of Architecture and Technology and Co-Director of Doctoral Programs at Harvard University Graduate School of Design. Trained as an engineer, architect, and historian of science and art, Picon is best known for his work in the history of architectural technologies from the eighteenth century to the present. He has published numerous articles and books in French and in English, mostly dealing with the complementary histories of architecture and technology. He has received a number of awards for his writings, including the Medaille de la Ville de Paris and twice the Prix du Livre d'Architecture de la ville de Briey.

Monica Ponce de Leon

Dean and Professor, Alfred Taubman College of Architecture and Urban Planning, University of Michigan

Monica Ponce de Leon is principal of the internationally known design firm, Office dA. She has held faculty professorships at Harvard Graduate School of Design, University of Miami, Northeastern University, and Georgia Institute of Technology, as well as many visiting professorships. She has received honors from the Architectural League of New York and the American Academy of Arts and Letters. Her practice has received numerous design awards. Among her authored works in the U.S. and international publications are works on topics ranging from Latin American architecture to eco-tourism to public infrastructure for the tropics.

Jonathan D. Solomon

Acting Head, Department of Architecture, The University of Hong Kong

Jonathan D. Solomon is an American architect based in Hong Kong. He is a founding editor of *306090* Books, a publication series featuring novel developments in architecture, landscape architecture and urbanism. His essays and criticism have appeared in publications worldwide. He is the author of *Pamphlet Architecture #26, 13 Projects for the Sheridan Expressway* (Princeton Architectural Press, 2004).